i

Riding The Bus 3

Riding The Bus 3
the dream continues

Luis Pástor

Riding The Bus 3

Copyright © 2012 Luis Pástor

All rights reserved.

ISBN:
ISBN-13:

Riding The Bus 3

CONTENTS

Alphabetical Contents	xviii
The Inspiration	xiv
Endorsements	xvi
Riding The Bus With Jesus	xviii
Antes de embarcar	xx
Avant d'embarquer	xxii
Mentions	xxiv
Dedication	xxviii
Acknowledgements	xxx
¡Dios, Dios, Dios!	1
"Givenaire"	2
13 Going On 30	3
21 Years	4
24 Horas	5
607	6
A New Beginning	7
Above All	8
April Showers	9
Awesome August	10
Beaux gens	11
Becoming A Father	12
Biarritz	13
Born Single	14
Bus Aerobics	15
Bus Driver	16
Bus Of Life	17
Bus Rider	18
Bus Writer	19
Cáncer	20
Cesar Chavez	21
Chasing The Bank	22
Chocolate Sundae	23

Clean The Soul	24
Descansar	25
Determined in December	26
Dryer	27
Everything Happens	28
Fabulous February	29
Five Dollars	30
Five Minutes	31
Five More Minutes	32
Fruitful Friday	33
Get Happy	34
God's Timing	35
Growth Through Subtraction	36
He Got Punished	37
Heavy Load	38
Hot Potatoes	39
Inventor	40
Is This Your Father?	41
It's So Easy	42
J'ai appris	43
Jammin' January	44
Je ne sais pas	45
Jovial June	46
July Jubilee	47
Juntos	48
Kency	49
La cuvette	50
Life	51
Línea 50	52
Look In Their Eyes	53
Lost And Found	54
Love Car #1	55
Love Car #2	56
Magical Bear	57

Memorable May	58
Mexicain-coreen-francais	59
Molino	60
Mon père francais –basque	61
Monumental Monday	62
More Accidents	63
Nania	64
Numerous November	65
Obvious October	66
Où se trouve la gare?	67
Prendre l'autbus	68
Primeras Lluvias	69
Rat's Race	70
Remember September	71
Riding The Bus With Jesus	72
Round #15	73
Running Again	74
Sacrifices	75
Sans amour	76
Satisfying Saturday	77
Sauna bus	78
Setbacks 3	79
She Cried	80
Singing Again	81
Start All Over Again	82
Terrific Tuesday	83
Test Of Fire	84
Thank You Lord	85
The Good Mexican	86
The Big 1 "0"	87
The Dream Continues	88
The Final Test	89
The Little Things	90
The Race Of Life	91

Thriving Thursday	92
Time To March	93
True To Yourself	94
Trust In The Lord	95
Two Wheelchairs	96
Un Champurrado	97
Un Milagro	98
Veinte Dólares.	99
Walk n'Roll	100
Waz Up Dawg?	101
What Would Jesus Do?	102
Who Are You?	103
Woman On The Floor	104
Wonderful Wednesday	105
About The Author	107

Riding The Bus 3

Riding The Bus 3

The Inspiration

Well this is number one and we're going to have some fun, ride me over, give me some hope do it again, write it over on my comp book, ride me over, give me a ride, do it again. Well this is number two and we're going to have some fun, ride me over, give me some hope do it again, write it over on my comp book, ride me over, give me a ride, do it again. Well this is number three and we're going to have some fun, buy my books, give me my dream, do it again, write it over on my comp book, buy me out, give YOU a dream, do it again. ☺

If there was a first one, a second one, then there has to be a third, especially of a good thing. Life continues to be a challenge but it is not the problems that matter, it is the "Dream", the solution. "Riding The Bus 3 – the dream continues" is just that. A relentless continuation of following one's dreams. Problems continue and new trials come but I keep riding the bus, saving money, praying, hoping, dreaming that tomorrow will be a better day, and it will. Anyone who goes through struggles in life has earned the right to give advice, and I take the privilege of pleading with you to look at life as beautiful

Riding The Bus 3 is the inspiration of others. I continue my quest to inspire those who are struggling and encourage those who are following the right path. My stories are your stories, your son's, your daughter's, your spouse's, your friends' and neighbors' stories. These stories are representative of the human quest to accomplish goals in life, to pursue happiness. Every experience is a fountain of wisdom and lessons for life.
.

Riding The Bus 3

Endorsements

At random, I met a teacher/poet who expressed some feelings for me about my dream to become an EMT in the Air force, Above All!
Isaiah, bus rider – future EMT.

This the most unique publication that we know about someone who rides the bus. Mr. Pástor's poetry is totally inspiring. His book enlightens our path. His poetry awakens the imagination in the reader and allows the author to reconnect with his own vital experience.
World Languages Department – Wilson High School.

I love Riding The bus 1 and 2. I cannot wait for book number three! Thank you to Mr. Luis Pástor for sharing your insightful and meaningful poems. When I read your poems I think about what life is all about. It makes me appreciate people, especially those who I think have nothing to teach me. But of course, I am wrong. Everyone has something to teach.
Alma Verdugo – Instructional Aide for the Deaf and Har of Hearing

Riding The Bus 1 and 2 are filled with poems about life that every person can relate to or be inspired by. It allows the reader to find the beauty in the simple things and to find strength in adversity. Thank you Mr. Luis Pástor for the wonderful poems and continue the great work!
Special Education Assistant and Future Teacher.
Lindsey Rangel

It was wonderful reading Mr. Pastor's Riding The Bus 1 and 2. His poems are very inspiring and heartfelt. I recommend his first and second book, and certainly his third upcoming book of dreams that can come true.
Rosie Aispuro – Special Ed Assitant

Riding The Bus 3

Riding The Bus 3

Riding The Bus With Jesus

In my enthusiasm to "hurry up and publish 'Riding The Bus 3 – the dream continues'" and trying to stay on schedule, I decided to publish a few poems that are exclusive to one of my future projects called "Riding The Bus With Jesus". When I say exclusive I don't mean that my readers need to be Christians to read my poems. What I mean is that my poetry is exclusive to Jesus and with a Christian message. Therefore, anyone can read my Christian poems that likewise send a message of hope and deliverance. I also own a Koran and a book called "God Is Not Great" by Christopher Hitchens. I want to learn about what others have to say.

With this sneak-peak I want to assure you that this work is not a judgmental approach. The purpose of my Christian poems is not to put down any organized religion or those who do not believe. I want to show candidly what I believe and the hope I hold in my heart. I know Jesus died for the sins of the world, rose on the third day, ascended into heaven and one day I will be with Him, whatever that may mean, it's all good for me.

I took some poems from my future project, "Riding The Bus With Jesus", that send a clear spiritual message. Nonetheless, I can't say that there are not more poems with incite about God in "Riding The Bus 3 – the dream continues". I share myself, my beliefs, and my ideas with my readers openly. Whenever I feel moved to put Jesus in a poem I do it. To avoid doing so would be to deny who I am. Please enjoy and grow as you journey through my inspirational poetry in motion.

Riding The Bus 3

xx

Antes de embarcar

Finalmente, tuve que comenzar a escribir poesía en español, mi lengua natal. Yo vivo en tres mundos lingüísticos. En mi escuela me comunico en español, francés e inglés. Me gusta la cultura y conocer gente de todas partes. El autobús es un lugar apto para lograr tal agrado. Por fin emprendí la meta de escribir literatura no solo para mis fanes de habla inglesa sino también de francófonos y de habla española.

Mis poemas en español son más reales, si pudiera decirlo así, porque en nuestra cultura vemos tamaleros, paleteros, y puestitos al borde de la calle. Nuestra cultura latina proviene de trabajadores y luchadores en la vida. La pobreza y la necesidad tiende a prevalecer en nuestras comunidades. Como latinos tenemos mucho que ofrecer al mundo: nuestro país, nuestra ciudad y nuestra comunidad. Pienso que los latinos estamos al borde de un gran éxito, por eso como profesor promuevo la educación de nuestra juventud.

Antes de comenzar su trayectoria por mis poemas, amigo, amiga, abra su mente, su imaginación y su corazón. Delante de usted encontrará la esperanza, la fe y tal vez un nuevo sueño. Lo último que muere es la esperanza decimos nosotros los latinos. Especialmente, aquellos latinos que saben sufrir - los campesinos, los trabajadores de fabricas. Todos ellos reconocen que en la vida se puede progresar cuando uno se lo propone. Yo lo sé, yo fui trabajador infantil en el campo y ahora, soy profesor. Les suplico que luchen conmigo por una vida mejor.

Riding The Bus 3

Avant d'embarquer

J'avais tellement envie de publier quelques-unes de mes idées et de mes poèmes en français, que je voulais aussi annoncer mon projet d'avenir de *Prendre l'autobus*. Je voudrais vous faire apprendre à découvrir un miracle qui se développait en même temps que l'économie baissait. Le miracle, le rêve continue malgré les problèmes et les obstacles. En vérité, il est presque impossible d'avancer sans friction, phénomène qui rend la vie plus intéressante.

Vous allez voir dans tous mes poèmes, en français, en anglais et en espagnol, que j'ai bataillé dans ma vie comme vous et comme tout le monde. Ce qui compte n'est pas que nous ayons eu des problèmes, mais que nous les ayons conquis. Vous verrez que mon cœur s'ouvre pour la vie, ma famille, mes étudiants, tous les gens en général, et bien sûr, j'ai une passion pour Dieu. J'ai beaucoup de gratitude envers mon père français/basque, la France et l'ensemble du monde francophone. Il faut surtout que le rêve continue et qu'il continue à jamais.

J'espère que vous aimerez tous mes poèmes en français, en espagnol et en anglais. Je voudrais que vous amélioriez votre propre vie en cherchant la passion qui soit particulière à votre vie. Je vous proposerez de nouvelles méthodes pour y penser. Je vous conseille aussi d'obtenir les autres livres (*www.createspace.com/4351776 et www.createspace.com/4263297*) pour avoir une image plus complète du rêve qui déferle vers le triomphe.

Riding The Bus 3

Mentions

M. Villalobos est sans aucun doute un homme qui m'inspire. Son expérience enrichit tous les livres qu'il a écrits et j'approuve et recommande tous les autres livres qu'il a l'intention de publier.
Marily Elizabeth – Cours de Français Avancé – 2014

J'étudie le français dans une cours avancé qu'enseigne M. Villalobos. Je voudrais recommander ses livres au monde entier car il a beaucoup d'inspiration et nous enseigne que nous pouvons surmonter tous les problèmes que nous avons dans ce monde.
Melissa Hernandez – Cours de Français Avancé – 2014

M. Villalobos a été mon professeur de français pendant trois ans. Ses livres sont passionnants et tout le monde devrait les lire. Or si vous ne les lisez pas, vous raterez une bonne occasion.
Samantha Hernandez – Cours de Français Avancé – 2014

La poésie elle-même est un moyen d'expression de soi, et bien, M. Villalobos exprime ses émotions en détails saisissants, en partageant ses expériences. En tant qu' élève pendant 4 ans, j'ai appris beaucoup de ses poèmes. Ils m'ont donné l'inspiration pour réussir et ne jamais lâcher mes rêves.
Jonathan Perez – Cours de Français Avancé – 2014

Dans ma classe de français, mon prof, M. Villalobos, nous lit ses poèmes inspirants qu'il a écrits au cours des dernières années. Il est un homme très sage qui vit non seulement pour lui mais pour ses élèves et il ne souhaite que le meilleur pour tout le monde, sans aucune doute dans ses poèmes.
Isaiah Salgado – Cours de Français Avancé – 2014

M. Villalobos est mon professeur de français avancé et ses poèmes nous inspire à réfléchir sur nos vies. Je recommande l'achat et des livres de M. Villalobos car sa poésie est très innovante ainsi qu'une source d'inspiration pour l'amateur de poésie.
Cristian Ramirez - Cours de Français Avancé – 2014

M. Pástor est un homme simple avec de grands rêves. Sa poésie vous ouvrira les yeux sur le monde dont vous avez rêvé et la personne que vous pouvez devenir.
Adrian Romero - Cours de Français Avancé – 2014

Cette poésie est très motivante et elle permet au lecteur de saisir de grands exemples de la vie réelle, d'événements réels. Je peux vraiment me connecter à ces poèmes. Ceux-ci donnent de conscil fondé sur des situations de la vie réelle. Je trouve la série de « Prendre l'autobus » fortement recommandé.
Anna Maria - Cours de Français Avancé – 2014

Riding The Bus 3

Riding The Bus 3

DEDICATION

I would like to dedicate Riding The Bus 3 – "the dream continues" first of all to my Lord Jesus and to the countless dreamers, friends, immediate family, extended family and supporters who continue to send words of encouragement my way. Anything that is worth anything requires much effort. I am going to put fourth all my effort in this work because some effort, some of the time is sometimes not enough.

Riding The Bus 3

xxx

ACKNOWLEDGMENTS

I would like to thank all my supporters: family, friends, students, colleagues , bus drivers and bus riders. The subtitle of my third book is the "dream continues". I show gratitude, to the stars, the cosmos, my God that I have not given up in spite of all the obstacles. Live the dream!

Riding The Bus 3

Riding The Bus 3

Riding The Bus 3

¡Dios, Dios, Dios! (1)

Mensaje: En la vida suceden momentos cuando uno simplemente tiene que acudir a Dios. Tal vez al principio nos creemos muy seguros de nosotros mismos pero llega momento cuando caemos en nuestras flaquezas. No siempre vamos a ser los fuertes, a veces tenemos que acudir a otros y a Dios. Esta historia se trata de una mujer que fue fuerte hasta que no pudo más. Quizá uno de nosotros pasamos por algo parecido o nos toca por padecer.

¡Dios, Dios, Dios! (1)

Estaba pasando tiempos muy difíciles
Miraba demonios, espíritus, peligro,
Acosada por la incertidumbre de la vida.

Corría sin dirección aterrorizada.
Sólo quería escapar de todo.
Su trayectoria la llevó lejos,
A un camino sin salida, un callejón.

¡Dios, Dios, Dios! gritaba desconsoladamente,
De allí salió sin haber encontrado a Dios.
Pero Dios sí la escuchó, allí estaba Él.

Ahora cuando yo paso por allí
Me gusta gritar, ¡Dios, Dios, Dios!
Ahora ese callejón es la expansión,
De la carretera, camino que Dios creó.

"Givenaire" (2)

Reflection: You know, money comes and goes. The money we don't use will not go with us when we die. The good deeds we do will. They are memories of the good things in life. When you have the opportunity to help someone, not only will you help them, but "you" will receive a blessing as well.

"Givenaire" (2)

I want a million dollars,
So that I can give a million.
I want to give to my wife,
My children, my students, myself.

I want to give to the Lord's Church,
The ten percent that is his.
Save ten percent for emergencies,
To live debt-free, pay cash only.

I want to have millions,
To help tens of thousands,
I know there are lots of needs,
Poverty, unemployment, drug addiction.

I want to give people their dream,
Their dream house, job, financial freedom.
"The poor shall be with you forever", Jesus said,
I want to be a "givenaire", so I can help.

13 Going On 30 (3)

Reflection: Some students love my poems so much that some have requested poems. This poem is not exclusive to one student but all students who aspire to do things in life. Nonetheless, one of my students, in my opinion resembles Jenna Rink, the main character of the movie "13 going on 30". Therefore, her story is the story of all students who aspire to accomplish goals in life.

13 Going On 30 (3)

Thirteen may be a turning point,
For many boys and girls,
They are discovering the world,
Many wish they could look older.

An unknown or uncertain world,
Of hopes and dreams is awaiting,
Where will a 13 year old be at age 30?
Will he/she be what he dreamed about?

What if they could fall asleep,
And wake up when they turned 30?
What if they could turn the clock back?
Maybe life would be better the second time.

Well, obviously we cannot do that,
So we better do what's right now,
"Jenna Rink, will you hit the screen again?"
When will you perform on 30 going on 100?

21 Years (4)

Moral: Divorce is an epidemic these days especially in the U.S. where we are hooked on statistics. Every day is a struggle to break with the status quo. The number 21 is magical for me. I am reminded of my second poem in Riding The Bus 1 "21 Ways To Say I Love You". My wife and I have made it to the 21 year mark.

21 Years (4)

21, a magical number,
The drinking, smoking age,
Three years after voting age.

I made it to 21 years!
Of loving my dear wife,
21 years of joy and struggles.

How much longer
Will the love sustain?
'Till death do us part,
Or debt do us part?"

It is easy to love,
When times are good,
Not so, during hard times.

For richer or poorer,
In sickness or in health,
How long? Time will tell.

24 Horas (5)

Moraleja: Una fresca mañana caminaba con calma hacia la parada del autobús sabiendo que podría llegar tarde. Me senté en la banca y comencé a observar y pensar. De repente me llamó la atención un signo que decía "OPEN 24 HOURS". Me vinieron recuerdos de tantas cosas que he logrado en la vida. Cuando se cierra una puerta se abre otra.

24 Horas (5)

La oportunidad está a la mano,
Sólo uno la tiene que buscar.
La prosperidad está a la vuelta
El camino hacia adelante.

Descasando, relajándome,
De repente comencé a soñar.
"ABIERTO 24 HORAS"
¿Qué está diciendo?

Por fin lo comprendí.
24 horas día y noche
El cosmos trabajando,
Ferviente a tu favor.

No te des por vencido
Sigue luchando por tus metas
Sigue soñando que puedes
Lo último que muere,

Es la esperanza.

607 (6)

Message: Whenever I miss the bus I always say that it is for a reason. Every time I miss something, I know I am gaining something else. I was sitting at the bench relaxing, not knowing the surprise that was awaiting. I was to meet the man and the service dog that would inspire my next poem.

607 (6)

If you're bored, ride the bus.
You'll see all kinds of stuff on the bus,
A man boarded the bus with a service dog.

Born on June 7th, 607 was his name.
The bipolar man named all his dogs,
By the month and day they were born.

"What does the dog do for you?", I asked.
"He keeps me calm, happy and content."
In time of need his best friend is there.

Well, I'm sure this is not the beginning or the end,
There are more stories, experiences up ahead,
Life, an endless fountain of thoughts and words.

Finally the bipolar rider arrived at his stop,
I asked if I could pet the friendly friend,
Then they walked into the sunset, on six legs.

A New Beginning (7)

Message: Whenever anyone thinks of their life, whether a child or an adult, sometimes it feels like an eternity. I have heard fourth graders call kindergarteners, little kids. I've heard high school students talk about the past like it was an eternity. When you become advanced in age, the past seems but a moment even though you have gone through a lot.

A New Beginning (7)

You're born, kindergarten, grammar school,
Junior high school, high school, college,
Every turn you make, you are starting over,

I began to think, life is full of changes,
Every step you take is a new beginning,
Every new beginning, adjustments must be made,

You got married, you became a parent,
Your children repeat everything all over again,
Finally they grow up and move away.

A new beginning for you and your children,
Now you know how your parents felt,
A new beginning for you and your spouse,

How long before the next new beginning,
Will there be a separation, divorce or death?
Will you become grandparents, awaiting the final step?

Above All (8)

Message: I love riding the bus, meeting all kinds of people. Recently I meet a young man, junior in high school, who has a dream to join the U.S. Are Force. He shared with me that his father was adamant about his goal but finally convinced him. The young junior showed me with pride the ASVAB test guide his father had given him.

Above All (8)

Remember I said,
You meet all kinds of people.
The bus is full of the young,
Old, married, single and students.

This time I met a student,
Who wants to go from the Metro,
To his dream of soaring the skies,
Look out Air Force, here I come!

He wants to be an EMT
An Emergency Medical Technician,
He wants to save the lives of his,
Fellow soldiers, unsung heroes.

No, he won't be a jar head,
He won't be a puddle pirate,
The air force didn't reject him yesterday,
Don't want to be called squid, semen.

He is the Chair Force, Above All!

April Showers (9)

Message: As I said before, thinking positive is a chore. Consequently, writing these poems is not easy. I feel that I am repeating myself and running out of words to say. Perhaps it's a good plus that I strive to be positive. The forces of negativism are much more stronger and prevalent. No one seems to mind that the F bomb is dropped every two or three words, in all parts of speech.

April Showers (9)

Maybe you thought the good old days,
Were over and downhill from here on.
But no, here comes April with its showers.
To shower you with blessings untold.

When you thought there was no more,
Hope for rain, a better future.
Then came the torrent rains,
Reminding you of the other side.

April showers to wash away,
The toil of March, the stress.
To remind you that May will be,
Better than ever before.

April, a month for reckoning,
Time to analyze triumphs, challenges.
From here on it only gets better.
The best is yet to come.

Awesome August (10)

Message: August is another month to be positive. August can be just as awesome as any other month. You can count up your triumphs and push forward with future plans. Don't give up, the year is not over yet. This time you may actually get what you have been working so hard to accomplish.

Awesome August (10)

You thought July was great?
August will be even better.
August will be awesome!

Come on now, you have to stay positive.
What's so good about August?
Children and teachers go back to school!

A new chance to do it right.
This school year will be better.
The old is past, trying new things.

August is the month of Augustus Caesar,
July for Julius Caesar, two emperors,
August is the month for conquerors.

What will you conquer this month?
What will you finally accomplish?
What will you keep trying to do?

Beaux gens (11)

Réflexion : Les stéréotypes ne sont pas bons. Il est injuste de juger toute une race basé sur le comportement d'un seule personne. Même s'il y a un grand nombre de personnes dans une catégorie on ne doit pas juger tous avec la même mesure. La plupart des français que j'avais la chance de rencontrer étaient très gentils avec moi. Etant que étranger, j'ai tous d'abord appris à parler la langue et je ne m'attendais pas qu'ils me parlaient dans ma langue.

Beaux gens (11)

On dit que les français,
Ne sont pas gentils,
Moi, j'ai vu le contraire,
A mon avis, les français sont très gentils.

J'avais dix-neuf ans, elle dix-sept ans,
Toutes sortes de personnes dans le transport,
Une fille française totalement étrangère,
Elle m'a montré Paris dans le métro.

Par tout j'avais de la chance,
La Pelouse, un restaurant/hôtel dont j'étais lave-vaisselle,
Une compagnie de construction où j'ai participé,
Dans l'œuvre d'une école et d'un centre de santé.

N'importe où, le métro, le travail, les magasins,
J'ai trouvé des peuples français gentils,
Qui voulaient seulement m'aider,
N'importe quoi, j'aime la France !

Becoming A Father (12)

Moral: Becoming a father is great responsibility. Anybody can bring life but not everyone can do it with style. Too many young men become fathers when they are not ready. Of those who are ready, these men find out that it is not an easy task to raise a child. I challenge all men, young and old, to become educated, go on the internet and learn how to be a great dad.

Becoming A Father (12)

Fatherhood, anyone can be a father,
But only a few can raise a child.
Anyone can have sex with anyone,
But only a man with integrity,
Will stay after the fun is over.

Teens becoming fathers, unemployed,
Lacking experience in life, no responsibilities,
Unprepared lacking role models,
Many are fatherless, single parent families,
It takes a miracle for a teen father to succeed.

Enough bashing teens, what about others,
How many grown men, after a divorce,
Neglect their children, don't provide support,
Whatever your age, don't neglect your children,
Don't grow up to be a dead-beat dad.

Biarritz (13)

Message : Quand j'étais ado la France était un paradis pour moi ou j'ai trouvé un endroit où je pouvais m'échapper la réalité, d'un monde qui ne marchait pas pour moi. Même aujourd'hui l'idée d'avoir la retraite en France, d'y aller chaque année me fascine. J'ai déjà fait quatre excursions éducatives avec mes étudiants, mais je voudrais y aller chaque année avec une cinquantaine d'étudiants.

Biarritz (13)

Les eaux verts, les peuple gentilles de l'Aquitaine,
La ville de mon père français, mon cœur,
J'étais la quand j'avais dix-neuf ans,
Et je suis retourné à l'âge de cinquante-trois.

Parfois je pense que j'habite,
Dans une ville qui n'est pas à moi.
Je aurais pu rester là,
Il y avait une fille qui m'aimait. ☺

Le Rocher de la Vierge, Hôtel du Palais,
La Chapelle, petite église de l'époque Byzantin.
Où je veux remarier ma belle femme.
Où je voudrais avoir ma retraite.

Mais j'ai besoin d'un miracle,
Il faut que je bénis des millions avec,
Riding The Bus 1, 2 et 3. Comme ça
Moi aussi je serai béni au-delà tous mesure.
Je ne vais pas oublier mon rêve et je ferai,
De grandes choses pendant la vie qui me reste.

Born Single (14)

Message: Sometimes it is really difficult to let go. I have heard and I have learned that if you really want something you have to let it go, and if it's yours, it will come back to you. If you love someone, let go, if you truly love him/her.

Born Single (14)

Naked I came into this world,
And naked I shall leave,
No, actually the mortician will dress me.

I will not take my savings,
I will not take my possessions,
Only what I give away will come back.

So if my wife dies first or she leaves me,
If I die, I will die single, like I was born,
If you truly want something, you gotta let go,

If you love your spouse, that's great!
If the love is not reciprocal, time will pass,
You had nothing when you were born.

You will take only the memories,
Of the good and the bad things you have done,
Remembering that you did your very best,

And that's all you can ask of yourself.

Bus Aerobics (15)

Reflection: At first glance we may judge someone who is standing at the bus stop stretching, running in place or doing arm rotations. But stop to think of all the money they are saving by working out at the bus stop. Recently I made a new friend called Arthr Itis. If you go past a bus stop and see an old Asian-looking man with a pony tail doing arm extensions and rotations, that would be me. ☺

Bus Aerobics (15)

The health spa, walking,
Running, lifting weights'
A little more creative,
Aerobics on the bus.

The same man running,
In place from Riding The Bus 1,
Pectoral muscles, defined calves,
Flexing muscles, toe lifts.

It's been two weeks,
Since I rode the bus,
I miss riding, writing,
Talking to riders, napping.

Bus aerobics, one of a kind.
Remembering the one hour,
All crumped up in the driver's seat,
Now, I'm going to stretch a little.

And take a well-deserved nap.

Bus Driver (16)

Message: We need to show appreciation for our community members: teachers, grocery store workers, peace officers, firefighters and yes, bus drivers. Bus drivers have built barricades to protect our President. Many have lost their lives by shooters and in traffic accidents. Many have been mistreated by riders and yet they keep driving. They are heroes. A few have even bought my books. ☺

Bus Driver (16)

This poem is dedicated,
To those unsung heroes,
Who day in and day out,
Are there to take you places.

Hail to these heroes who,
Who gave their lives,
In the line of duty.

Hail to those bus drivers
With great personalities,
Who greet you with a smile.

I know there are bad ones too,
They are humans just like us.
Thank God I don't have to drive.
Instead I write and then take a short nap.

Thank God for bus drivers!

Bus Of Life (17)

Message: The public bus transports all kinds of people: infants, teens, woman, elderly, homeless, students, librarians, teachers, business people, toddlers, the mentally ill, everyone! You cannot meet this gamut of people in the privacy of your car. On the bus you rub shoulders with the best of the best and sometimes, the worst of the worst. There is not a boring day on the bus but if you are bored, just take a nap. ☺

Bus Of Life (17)

Life is a journey,
Goin' places, doin' things,
I think of people and their lives,
Some get on, some get off.

Where will the bus go?
Where is everyone going?
Life has so many twists and turns,
What will happen down the road?

The bus of life, bus 76,
People talking, the music of voices,
Spanish, English, Mandarin, Cantonese…
The stories of the multitude.

Stop and go like life itself,
Talk and sleep, write and read,
Think about my life,
Wondering what life will bring.

Bus Rider (18)

Message: I dedicated a poem to bus writers, people who write on the bus, bus driver, the hero for commuters, and of course I have something to say about those dedicated "bus riders". Those bus riders who are so dedicated that they belong to the Bus Riders Union.

Bus Rider (18)

To those relentless riders,
Who by choice or necessity,
Board limos, that's what I call them,
Buses that take people places.

Committed riders who have discovered,
The beauty of public transportation,
Who help keep our air clean.

Defending Title VI of the 1964 Civil Rights Act
Fighting against massive hikes in bus fares,
Advocates for clean air in big cities.

Fighting courageously for the rights of the poor,
I need to step up to the plate and join,
Need to join those who are willing to make a change,
Making changes for the good of all.

Bus Writer (19)

Message: If you have a dream you have to keep working for it. My dream is to be known as the bus writer of bus riders, as a friend once described me. If I want this dream, I have to keep writing and I have to keep riding. The moment I stop working, that's when the dream is lost. But even then, I can get up and start all over again.

Bus Writer (19)

A bus buddy once called me,
The bus writer of bus riders.
Riding, writing, sleeping, relaxing.

Sometimes I'll stop to talk,
To my avid poetry supporters.
Sharing my favorite poems.

Writing my past, present, and future.
The wheels of the bus to my destiny,
My lucky pen scratching away.

I feel sleepy now, my eyes
Slow dancing to the purring of my cat,
The soothing music of the bus.

Cáncer (20)

Reflexión: El cáncer como muchas otras enfermedades acaba con la vida de las víctimas aun antes de la muerte. El dolor que causa la quimioterapia puede ser intolerante. Perder partes del cuerpo puede ser devastador. Yo pienso que la enfrenta con las desventuras de la vida es la única forma de ganar. Algo malo puede ser transformado en algo bueno si uno se lo propone.

Cáncer (20)

El cáncer no es una enfermedad.
Es el casamiento de dos idiomas
"can' que significa puedo
Y la palabra mal escrita, "cer"

Yo propongo un neologismo, "canser".
Que demuestra que luchar
Por lo que uno quiere en la vida,
Es el único camino.

Yo "canser" el que refugie a niños huérfanos.
Yo "canser" el que estudie para doctor.
Yo "canser" el que encuentre la cura
Para las enfermedades mortales.

En la vida nos encontramos,
Con problemas que nos destruyen,
Que nos quitan la esperanza,
Y eso depende como lo vemos.

Cesar Chavez (21)

Moral: Recently I went to watch the new release of Cesar Chavez. This movie brought back memories of the struggles my family endured as farm workers. I learned things about Cesar Chavez that I never imagined, such as his travels to Europe to stop the sale of California grapes and negotiate with British and Scandinavian labor unions.

Cesar Chavez (21)

A true modern day hero,
Who sacrificed, who was not selfish,
Who traveled the uncharted road.

Was willing to go as far as needed,
Stopped feeding himself to call attention,
Leading to illness that finally took his life.

Nixon supporting the table grape growers,
The grape growers and wineries,
Thought they had won the war.

But Chavez was willing to travel across the ocean,
To win the hearts of European labor unions,
California grapes would not be sold in Europe.

The humble beginnings of simple man,
Who would not give up, no matter what,
An icon for anyone with a dream!

Chasing The Bank (22)

Message: Chasing The Bank is a continuation of Chase Bank, one of my favorite poems of Riding The Bus 1. It talks about the importance of saving money for emergencies. Too many Americans, including myself, have used credit as emergency money. Without realizing it we were only digging a deeper hole for ourselves. Many families were disintegrated during the current economic downfall for lack of savings for emergencies.

Chasing The Bank (22)

It's been over three years now,
Since I started riding the bus,
Three years ago I sold my Tacoma,
To pay off my wife's Chrysler.

Now it's my dream to put money,
In the bank to be my own banker.
It hasn't been easy at times,
But my dream to be free continues.

Instead of paying 300 per month,
I want to save 300 per month,
Instead of buying new on credit,
Buy used, pay cash, save money.

Instead of paying to drive,
I want to be paid for not driving,
Chasing the bank to save for emergencies,
To enjoy life in freedom, the stress of debt.

Chocolate Sundae (23)

Message: Like any day of the week, Sunday can be a great day to be positive. The alternative is not very appetizing. We humans spend too much time complaining about things we cannot change and worrying about things that will never happen. It takes effort and a great amount of energy to look at life from a positive point of view. Nevertheless, it is well worth the effort and the reward.

Chocolate Sundae (23)

Finally, the first or the last day
Of the week, depending on your beliefs.
A day to be with family, go to church,
A day to reflect and seek the Truth.

Time to get a Chocolate Sundae!
Sunday, "Funday" for family and friends.
Time to relax, nap, read a good book.
Maybe my series of "Riding the Bus". ☺

A day to start fresh, to keep dreaming,
Making plans for the coming week,
A day to evaluate yourself, your life,
Take time off just to think.

The first or the last day of the week,
Is finally here to promise a better tomorrow,
The first chance and the last chance,
To do things the right way.

Clean The Soul (24)

Message: As men and women, boys and girls go through life, more than once they have to cry. As we grow older, people tell us not to cry especially if you are male. That's what society says. Anybody who does not admit a weakness, and believes himself to be strong, may never have the courage and tears to make the change.

Clean The Soul (24)

Soap cleans dishes, clothing, your body,
The rain cleans the streets, the air,
And tears clean your face, your soul.

You lost your spouse?
You failed your test again?
Let your tears pick you up again.

You keep trying and trying?
You can't seem to make headway?
Your tears give you the strength to go on.

You know? Life is a series,
Of twists and turns, ups and downs,
Ride the waves of your tears.

People say that tears,
Are a sign of the weak.
But you know you are strong.

Descansar (25)

Moraleja: Hace poco escribí un poema llamado "24 Horas" donde di a entender que las oportunidades nunca dejan de existir 24 horas al día. Y sí es cierto que debemos tener confianza, trabajar y pensar que algo bueno está por venir. Por otra parte la mucha ambición por tener más cosas materiales puede ser dañina. Trabajar largas horas para pagar las tarjetas que usamos, irresponsablemente, para comprar cosas que no eran necesarias puede acabar con nuestra salud. Descansa, ahorra y compra sólo lo que te alcanza to dinero efectivo.

Descansar (25)

La economía está decayendo.
El restaurante de 24 horas está cerrado.
Antes dije que las oportunidades
Existen 24 horas al día.

¿Será que ahora Dios está descansando?
¿Será que la gente de la noche,
Ya no gasta su dinero como antes?
¿Habremos aprendido la lección?

En caso de que esté descansando,
También yo voy a descansar.
Es bueno tener metas y sueños,
Pero no a tal extremo de no relajarse.

Yo he aprendido la lección.
Que el uso irresponsable del crédito,
Es una enfermedad que arrasa,
Con la gente, la paz, la economía.

Determined December (26)

Reflection: I can't believe it! It was a difficult task to stay positive throughout the days of the week and the months of the year. It is like life itself. It is no easier to write 19 positive poems than it is to live life in a positive way. Therefore, I encourage you to live life fervently no matter what may happen in your life.

Determined December (26)

The last month of the year,
The last chance to do things right,
To finish the year with a bang.

I am determined to make December,
The end of a great year, to make it count,
To prepare for the upcoming year, 2014.

I am determined to accomplish my goals,
Determined to start new projects, improve,
To make this month count for all.

Some celebrate the birth of Jesus,
Others reserve this time for family gatherings,
Whatever the case, make December count.

Make December a month to remember,
Just like September, October, and November,
Great things to come in December.

Dryer (27)

Moral: The fallen economy is getting the best of most people. We have been trained since children that money is magic. We can get money out of a credit card or the ATM, like a slot machine at the casino. People may not be able to afford a new dryer, but they get a new one now and think that they can pay it later.

Dryer (27)

I finally learned the value of money,
Money does not grow on trees or plastic,
Adults think money grows on plastic,
That's why we run up our credit to divorce.

Don't get me wrong, money does grow,
But does your bank account grow?
Or do your credit aches and pains grow?
Have you spent so much that you went over?

Our 1500 dryer finally broke down,
Conveniently after the warrantee expired,
My wife wanted a new one, and we were broke,
I was committed to walk away from credit.

I had 50 dollars set aside for a dryer,
Thank God for the bargains at the flea market,
My state of the art jewel, good over two years now,
I will not let credit dry out my savings.

Everything Happens (28)

Message: Have you ever met up with the same person more than once, in the least likely of places? Have you wondered why you have crossed paths so many times? Things happen for a reason, though we may never know, rest assured, it's all in the mix.

Everything Happens (28)

I was a teacher aid at a junior high school,
Went back to college, two years later,
I found a job at a local high school,
In both cases, she was there.

Moved to teach in Los Angeles,
My aunt from Mexico City.
Was visiting, she called me to meet her,
At the airport, and my student was there.

Twenty years later, my friend from fifth grade,
Having dinner, reminiscing, my son at my side,
There was a beautiful woman across from me,
I looked at her, she looked at me, suddenly,

She walked over to me and greeted me,
I didn't recognize her at first, it was her,
She was all grown up, high school Spanish teacher,
She made it, she pursued her dream!

Everything happens for a reason, who knows?
What that reason might be, it's a mystery.

Fabulous February (29)

Reflection: Ok, my poetry is about being positive so I have to find something special to say about February. Not a difficult task when we consider that February 29th happens every four years to compensate for the leap year. Every four years, February offers us one extra day to accomplish fabulous things. If you were born on February 29th it would be nice if you could age four years slower than everyone else. When you turned 25, your best friend would be 100 years old!

Fabulous February (29)

This is exciting!
We're off to a good start.
Jammin January is gone,
Fabulous February here to stay.

This is the month of fabulous,
Great ideas, to get things done.
This is the time for new plans,
Things can only get better.

February, my sanctuary,
Not an ordinary month,
Step two of the new year.
Not a month to give up.

If you were born in February,
You are lucky, especially if
Your birthday is the 29th,
Others age, you, forever young. ☺

Five Dollars (30)

Moral: Believe it or not, I am not interested in money, I don't believe it either. Even if I loved money somewhere in my subconscious mind I would still not be able to take any amount of money when I die. Even if I realized my dream to become a "givenaire", I wouldn't be able to take one penny with me to the grave. I wouldn't know that a parade of paid limos were following me. Nonetheless, I am going to request local buses to transport my body and my paid (just kidding) ☺ mourners.

Five Dollars (30)

What is the value of money?
How much is five dollars?
How far can your money go?

"Excuse me sir, I love your poems,
But I can't afford your book,
I live on SSI and I barely make it
Can I have it for five dollars?"

I looked at him with a smile,
"Well sir, this book costs ten dollars,
I wanted to take it to the grave."

My fans let out a laugh.
Of course I can't take the money,
To my final journey, my destination.
So what is the value of five dollars?

Five Minutes (31)

Reflection: Look it's ok to feel sorry for yourself, for a while. During a time when I was having second thoughts about my goals, counting the costs, I came up with the idea that I should take five minutes off to feel sorry for myself. I put the alarm on my phone for five minutes and vowed to get up and keep going again.

Five Minutes (31)

Sometimes minutes, hours, and days,
May drag when times are hard.
Give yourself permission to be sorry,
For yourself and your challenges.

Take five minutes to complain,
To think of all the things that,
Could be better, improve, be resolved.
Imagine a life without cares and worries.

Take a five minute break
To list all your mishaps,
To lament the things that went not,
That could have been.

Put the timer on, don't go past,
Get ready to take a new turn.
Your alarm is the trumpet of triumph.
Announcing the replacement of strife for victory.

Five More Minutes (32)

Reflection: After conducting my five minute "feel sorry for myself therapy" I became inspired to write the continuation: Five More Minutes. I realized that there had to be part two of my therapy treatment. I thought that it was just as important or perhaps more important to spend the next five minutes counting my blessings.

Five More Minutes (32)

Ok, you felt sorry for yourself,
Great! Now let's take the next five minutes,
To be thankful for what I have.

For starters, be thankful for your,
Arms, legs, hands, feet, eyes, nose…
There is so much to be thankful for.

If you have a spouse, son, daughter,
If you have a house, two dogs, and a cat,
Be thankful for what you have.

I know life is not perfect.
There are problems, but see them as challenges.
Life would be boring without friction.

So make a list of hundreds,
Of things you can be thankful for,
Think positive and think big!

Fruitful Friday (33)

Reflection: It is not easy to think positive. Sometimes we have to force ourselves to find the good in things. Our natural tendency is to expect the worst; not a day of progress but frightful Friday. I challenge myself and my readers to forcedly find the positive side of life.

Fruitful Friday (33)

Apples, oranges, mangos, pears…
So many fruits to think about.
Bananas, peaches, grapes, guavas,
Why think about your problems?

For many people, Friday is the last day,
Of a hard and tedious week of work,
Can't wait for the end of the week,
To rest, to relax, catch up, work at home.

I propose that every day of the week is great!
Enjoy today, looking forward to tomorrow.
Just like Fruitful Friday, full of hope,
Saturday, another day to enjoy, to accomplish.

I've heard it say that an apple a day
Can keep the doctor away, but,
An onion a day will keep everybody away.
Fruits, nuts and berries, Friday, all the same.

Get Happy (34)

Message: Money is not everything in life, but it helps. Nonetheless, we should not make money our priority. When we die, we will not take a penny with us, but we will remember when we tried to help someone and the satisfaction we received. More important than money is that you enjoy what you do, and help someone along the way. I love writing my "poetry in motion" and I hope someone will be blessed through my efforts.

Get Happy (34)

Riding the bus, writing poetry,
Relaxing, sleeping, correcting papers,
Sharing my poetry, selling my books.

Having fun composing stories,
Sharing my thoughts with strangers,
Dreaming that I will be great!

In more than one occasion,
I have given a book away,
To a poor, needy rider.

Before I hand the book over,
I sign it and tell them the cost,
"I planned to take these 10 dollars to the grave."

They turn to me and smile,
I may not get rich with my books,
But sure enough, I'll get happy. ☺

God's Timing (35)

Moral: Sometimes in life we want things right now! and our way. Maybe we depend on the internet or little gadgets to help keep us on track. This morning I forgot my cell phone. I usually set the alarm to sound every five minutes to pace myself. This morning I heard the Lord's voice (not literally) tell me that I had to depend on his timing, not on my cell phone.

God's Timing (35)

Sometimes when we think
We are ahead of the game,
Really we are behind our mark.

Sometimes we think,
We will not make it,
But the Lord is watching our step.

It only takes an accident,
To slow us down, to be late,
Or someone else's fate will give us favor.

Forgetting my cell phone,
Reminded me that I am on God's timing,
I might just miss the bus anyway.

Cell phone or not,
I am on God's timing.
"Thank you Lord", as I board

My "limo" on time.

Grow Through Subtraction (36)

Moral: Pastor Jim Reeve of Faith Community Church in West Covina, California is an anointed preacher of the Word of God. During the past year he has made me cry, laugh, and even get angry. The Word of God becomes alive and practical during his sermons. "Grow through subtraction" is a concept he has shared with the church more than once. This concept makes me think of the many things I lost in life and how I grew from losing..

Grow Through Subtraction (36)

The rose bushes in my backyard,
Were recently pruned, shedding dead branches,
I began to think of the beautiful roses,
That will come from a short stump.

I turned my attention to my trees,
Recently trimmed, blossoms reappearing,
My fruit trees must shed their fruit,
To feed others, rid themselves of the weight.

Then I began thinking of myself,
What do I need to cut back?
What weighs so much on my limbs?
That I refuse to let go and give away?

Thinking back, I've lost a lot,
And those lessons brought other opportunities,
"Cut back un my pride, fear, distrust, Lord.
So I can bring forth power, love and hope."

He Got Punished (37)

Moral: I've talked about my life as a farmworker before. It was my bread and butter. My mother's income was not enough to feed all of us and my father had gone back to Tijuana to take care of his mother. When I was about 14 years old, I saw an Anglo boy picking tomatoes in the distance. I had to go up to him and learn the scoop.

He Got Punished (37)

The teen years had arrived,
I wanted to be going to the movies,
Going to summer camp like the rich kids.

Instead, I was out in the scorching sun,
Picking tomatoes, picking my nose,
Wiping the sweat off my forehead,
When a white boy caught my attention.

I was intuitive, I had to find out why he was there,
"A Yellow Submarine" blasting from his transistor,
Why are you picking tomatoes like us?

I began to wonder what he would say,
Was he poor like us, did his father die?
No, his father owned the ranch, he was punished,
Man, I do this for a living!

I knew then, I had to go to college.

Heavy Load (38)

Message: There is a lot of poverty in the world. In Southern California you don't need to go to 4th street to see poverty, all you need to do is ride public transportation. In the time I have ridden the bus I have seen people with large baskets, humongous luggage, and now two large laundry bags. A large bag of clothing can be very heavy.

Heavy Load (38)

An elderly couple boarded the bus,
With two large bags of laundry.
I began to think of the poverty
That haunts the streets of Los Angeles.

What is this elderly couple doing?
Lugging to large cumbersome bags,
Filled with clothing, on route to,
The laundry mat, to clean away the grime.

Can't they afford a car?
Can't the neighbors take them for a ride?
Why are some people so poor?
How do people come to this point?

I began to think about the heavy load,
That people carry throughout their lives,
Much heavier that two large laundry bags,
Lord, help me carry this heavy load.

Hot Potatoes (39)

Message: I have found that my books sell best when I ask people if they would want my books. I don't want to pay for advertisement because there is no guarantee that my books will sell. I don't believe in investing if I can't afford it. I have to have the cash on hand. I want to teach people that credit is an evil in our society that is destroying our economy.

Hot Potatoes (39)

I was wondering when,
My books would start selling again,
It was a matter of time,
They're selling like hot potatoes.

At the bus stop, on the bus,
At work, at karate lessons, on the street,
Goes to show, should never give up,
The dream is unfolding.

Taking the bus, taking my books,
My hand on my heart, hoping,
To find someone to bless, bless me back,
To show me that dreams come true.

You can't hold a hot potato for too long,
You have to let go, it will burn you.
I want my books to be like hot potatoes,
To put one in everyone's hands.

Inventor (40)

Message: I like meeting people who have dreams and express their dreams. In a way I think everyone has a dream or had a dream but perhaps they didn't pursue it fervently. I don't think it is enough to just be alive, there has to be life in your life. If you don't have a dream get one and don't stop until you accomplish it.

Inventor (40)

I told you once before,
And I'll tell you again,
All kinds of people on the bus.

Now, I finally met an inventor,
A very private inventor, will not give a clue,
Something that every bus rider must want.

She speaks often about her idea,
Has her fans wondering, guessing,
Is it a magic pillow, Swiss army backpack?

One day her invention will materialize.
My Riding The Bus series will finally triumph.
Both of us, dedicated riders who never gave up.

I hope her invention is a cure all,
For the ailments and problems of the world,
Every bus rider, my book and her invention on hand.

Is This Your Father? (41)

Reflection: The Bible says, "Wisdom screams out in the streets." Basically, if you want wisdom you can find it anywhere and everywhere. This retired gang member knew how hard life can be without the guidance of a father. This "veterano" gave my son advice that was real, a man who lived what he was talking about.

Is This Your Father? (41)

"Excuse me, little boy,
Is that your father?
Is this your son, sir?"

"Man, I wish my father
Rode the bus with me
When I was a child,
He was in jail!"

This "veterano" gave my son,
The advice of a life time.
He saw the value of fatherhood.

I began to think of my life,
Having grown up without a father,
I envied my best friend for his father.
How many children are in need of a father?

If you are a father, listen to this story.
Someday you will be a father, be the best.
In a divorce, a one night stand, you are still a father.

It's So Easy (42)

Message: I feel like I am repeating myself too much. Yet at the same time, I cannot talk about being positive enough. We live in a society where mishaps are more popular than good news. Bad news and violence sells a lot more than every day good living. You may do 1000 good things in your life but you may not make the front page until you commit a crime. I have to keep pushing and selling and giving people hope.

It's So Easy (42)

Things don't always turn out,
The way we planned them.
Not always do I get,
What I want, the way I want it.

My students are not performing
To the best of their ability.
Financial problems and other challenges
Continue to push, to bring me down.

It's so easy to give up,
Anybody can give up any time.
Only a few can wait it out,
Long enough to the final battle.

Don't give up, it's too easy!
Great things take time to mature.
I've heard it said that it's ok,
To lose a few battles, but win the war.

J'ai appris (43)

Message : La personne qui a peur a trouvé son ennemi le plus dangereux. La peur nous empêche de réaliser nos rêves. Moi, je savais nager et je pouvais nager mais la peur faisait que mon corps se figeait. Lorsque j'étais petit on m'a fait peur à la plage et cela a contribué d'une façon a développer un sentiment d'insécurité. La France a été l'unique endroit où je me sentais plus apte à prendre des risques.

J'ai appris (43)

Si on a peur, il est difficile,
De faire les choses importantes dans la vie,
Les choses ne peuvent pas s'effectuer,
La peur est l'ennemie du succès.

Les belles filles étaient sur le point d'arriver,
Nous étions à la piscine municipale du quartier,
« Elles vont se rigoler de nous ! », disaient mes amis.
« Il sera nécessaire que vous me jetiez là-dedans.

Ils m'ont pris des mains et des pieds,
Et ils m'ont lancé vers l'eau,
J'étais si content en France,
Que j'avais toute confiance en eux.

Je suis sorti de l'eau comme un poisson,
J'ai appris que la peur est l'ennemie du succès,
Dans la vie la peur peut nous vaincre, peur de l'eau,
Depuis ce moment-là, je nage comme un poisson.

Jammin January (44)

Reflection: January is a sacred month for most cultures. The Western World and the Americas all celebrate New Year's Day. January marks a new beginning when many commit to a new year's resolution. Whatever your culture or whenever you celebrate a new beginning do it with fervor. As long as you have hope, there is always a chance that things will get better.

Jammin January (44)

New Year's Day, New Year's resolutions.
High hopes and dreams, promises made.
This year will be definitely better.
Things started last year will be completed.

It takes time to accomplish goals,
January is your jumpstart.
Have to keep trying, can't give up.
The good things in life take time.

So let's get a good start!
Pace yourself and set goals.
For every negative thought,
Conjure up three positive thoughts.

Well, January is just like December.
The beginning is the end all over again.
Don't worry, it's a sure thing,
Another chance, to do it better this time.

Je ne sais pas (45)

Je vous prie de m'excuser. Cette chanson, ce poème ne déborde d'optimisme ☹. Je sais, la vie n'est pas juste. C'est pour cela qu'on doit se pousser pour être positif ☺.

Je ne sais pas (45)

Je ne sais pas,
Ce que je ferai sans toi,
Je suis habitué à toi.

Non, non, non, non,
Je ne sais quoi viendra,
Si tu me laisses comme ça.

J'essaierai,
De t'oublier,
Les jours de notre bonheur.

Même si tu es,
Effacée de ma mémoire,
Mon cœur se rappellera de toi.

Reviens à moi,
Ne me fais pas souffrir,
Regarde-moi,
Je suis tout seul sans toi,
Je ne peux même pas sourire.

Jovial June (46)

Look, you don't need an excuse to be happy. Just so happens that jovial somewhat rhymes with June. Any month of the year can be great, it all depends how we see the world. If this is the month of June for you and you are going through a hard time, just remember to be jovial. There is a solution for your problem, you just have to keep looking.

Jovial June (46)

I know the weather might
Get really hot in June,
Really humid and undesirable.

Nevertheless, there is a lot to be
Happy about in jovial June,
Farmers rejoice at harvest time.

Fruits and vegetables ripen on the vine.
Flowers blooming everywhere,
Eager to drink the chlorophyll of the sun.

Hot weather can be a surfer's dream,
Catching the waves at dawn, I don't
Do that, but it must be cool.

So it depends how you look at things,
What you like to do in the hot or cold,
There's a season for everything, I know.

July Jubilee (47)

Reflection: July is the month of celebration. The United States and France celebrate their independence. We are over half way through the year. This would be a great time to reflect on the current year's accomplishments and figure out what we learned through the shortcomings. Look at life with a microscope and you will find a lot to celebrate in your own life.

July Jubilee (47)

4th of July, 14th of July.
Probably other countries
Celebrate their independence in July.

For me, I'm celebrating in July,
Just because I'm alive!
Simply 'cause I'm a lucky guy.

You too. Think of all that,
You can celebrate in your life,
I'm sure you've had good times.

It's easy to get depressed,
It's hard work to get happy sometimes,
You choose, celebrate or complain?

July is the month of Jubilee,
To celebrate all you have accomplished,
To remember the day of victory!

Juntos (48)

Mensaje: Estamos viviendo en una época donde las promesas están perdiendo su valor. En particular, los matrimonios están cayendo bajo las fuerzas del tiempo, la economía y el olvido del compromiso. En un momento nos sentimos solos y sin fuerzas para seguir. Buscamos una persona que nos pueda alentar en la vida. Voltea y mira, esa persona todavía está a tu lado, quien puede seguir siendo tu colaboradora/colaborador.

Juntos (48)

Cuando la gente se une,
Se puede uno realizar mejor,
Lavar platos con alguien,
Puede ser más divertido, por ejemplo.

Todos trabajamos mucho,
Todos estamos cansados, presionados,
Pero mantener una casa limpia,
Juntos, puede ser divertido.

La economía está decayendo,
El ánimo y la esperanza, disipando.
Pero, juntos podemos pagar,
Más pronto, los errores del pasado.

Juntos podemos emprender un negocio,
Juntos hemos criado dos hijos,
Juntos hemos sobresalido,
En la misma cripta, juntos quedaremos.

Kency (49)

Moral: These kinds of things you cannot plan, they just happen but you have to be ready to take it all in. My heart dropped to the floor when I saw them walk in together: my two best students, I loved them both the same. Since God gave me two arms I took the liberty of hugging them both at the same time. I saw the miracle of leaving things in the hands of God. All I did was pray, I had faith and I let it go.

Kency (49)

Wow! There is so much to say!
Hope, love, forgiveness
True friendship forever.

There came a time when they couldn't see
They couldn't see what was being lost
But time is the healer of all.

I left it in the hands of God
Forgot and remembered from time to time
Then the big day came.

She had the "morales" (morals) to apologies
A fusion of love and forgiveness between two girls
And a new name is born: Kenia + Nancy = Kency

Her firstborn daughter will be named Kency.

La cuvette (50)

Réflexion : Parfois, l'humeur français peut être un peu fort. Je crois que les français sont un peu plus honnêtes et naturels. Ils n'ont pas peur de parler de toilettes, de sexe, de politique, de tout. La France est un peu plus libérale peut-être, je crois. Je ne veux pas utiliser un stéréotype pour toute la France. Cela ne serait pas juste.

La cuvette (50)

La cuvette est un endroit spécial,
Où on peut se reposer, penser profondément,
On peut lire, parler au portable,
Envoyer des textes, aller sur Facebook.

Mais jamais tu n'as pas imaginé
Que tu pourrais t'asseoir sur,
Une cuvette en forme de main.

Ça m'est arrivé à moi à Bayonne, France.
Un ami avait une cuvette, main de porcelaine,
Jamais je n'avais vu telle chose.

J'étais si intéressé que j'ai cherché sur Internet,
J'ai trouvé des tasses de café en forme de toilette,
J'ai trouvé des urinoirs en forme de bouche,
Dégoûtant ! Je n'aurais pas raconté cette histoire,
Mais crois-moi, c'était vraiment rigolo !

De m'asseoir sur une cuvette en forme de main. ☺

Life (51)

Reflection: Generation after generation people have come gone and have gone. My wife and I used to have a flea market business. My wife would go to Good Will and buy carts of used items. No one knew what we would find. Occasionally, we would find complete family albums. I would stop to think that my family pictures may end up in a flea market 100 years from now.

Life (51)

Life will take its course,
Battles will be lost,
And wars will be won.

Life can be a game,
To be played by the rules,
To be played with skill and audacity.

Life can be a challenge,
Bigger than our strength, our desire,
It can knock down the strongest.

Life is journey to the unknown,
It has twists and turns, ups and downs,
Must have a road map, avoid getting lost.

The funny thing about the game of life,
After the struggles, the challenges,
No one gets out alive. ☺

Línea 50 (52)

Mensaje: Si andas buscando un milagro lo puedes encontrar donde menos lo esperabas. Lo importante es que nunca dejes de perseguir tu sueño. Tal es la historia de esta pareja que se encontró en el mismo autobús. Quizá la vida es así, las cosas buenas las encuentras en tu camino. Ya está de ti si escoges el camino del amor.

Línea 50 (52)

En el autobús se conoce
Todo tipo de gente,
Flacos, gordos, feos, bonitos,
Niños, niñas, ancianos, ancianas
Y por fin, hasta un amor.
Se puede encontrar en él.

Se equivocaron ambos de línea,
O tal vez no fue un error.
Ni él ni ella debían de haber
Tomado la línea cincuenta.
Cada uno tenía su propio camino,
Y terminaron en un mismo destino.

Algunos critican la transportación pública,
Pero yo soy testigo de un amor,
Nacido donde uno menos lo esperaba,
Ya tienen hijos, ya tienen nietos,
Bodas de Plata. Yo quiero estar presente,
Cuando lleguen las Bodas de Oro.

Look In Their Eyes (53)

Moral: Marriage can be very challenging. If there are children involved it can be very difficult. A friend told me of a couple that would fight in the presence of their children and would not stop to think the harm they were causing. In one occasion my friend confronted the couple and told them that they would stop fighting if only they looked in their children's eyes.

Look In Their Eyes (53)

It is amazing how most marriages,
Begin kissy, kissy, with great expectations.
Soon they become the war of all nations.

The children would run and hide,
Screams coming from Mom and Dad,
The dream and promises forgotten.

Economic and social troubles rising,
Extended family meddling in affairs,
If only they looked in their eyes.

Tensions rising, talk of divorce,
If they looked in their children's eyes,
They wouldn't scream and fight anymore.

Mom and Dad look in each other's eyes too,
The windows of your partner's heart.
Look inside, you'll find love and hope.

Lost And Found (54)

Moral: How many times have you lost something and found it. I have been very lucky in this aspect. I lost my wallet with money, in Paris, France and I found it. Someone had turned it in at the main bus station. Recently, I lost my bus pass and my computer, both recovered. In all these cases I prayed and asked God for a miracle.

Lost And Found (54)

What a terrible feeling,
To lose something of value,
Loss of money, time and effort.

I lost my wallet
And an angel saved me,
From financial hardship.

I lost my laptop, ran back,
Retracing my steps, it was safe and sound,
On a bench right where I left it.

I lost my bus pass,
An honest bus driver,
Had the heart to save it.

Losing and winning is part of life,
I lost my temper, Lord,
Hope I never find it again.

Love Car #1 (55)

Moral: Sometimes when you think you are finished with something, you really are not. Emergencies are emergencies, that's why they call them emergencies. I wasn't prepared to buy a car cash because I had just finished paying my debt. Nevertheless, I am going to start all over again, I have to if I want to win.

Love Car #1 (55)

I had finally finished,
Paying off my debt,
When love stepped in.

Love can stop anyone,
Right in their tracks,
To reflect one more time.

The emergency came,
And I wasn't prepared,
My son needed his dad.

Love car #1 on credit,
I am going to start all over again,
For the sake of the dream.

Love Car #2 (56)

Message: Credit is an evil that is destroying our economy, I said it once and I will say it again. I believe that we are not dealing with real money for the most part. Your average citizen to the largest corporations can declare bankruptcy and nothing seems to be lost. Where does that money come from? Why do people come back so fast from a bankruptcy? Think about it.

Love Car #2 (56)

The economy keeps chasing me around,
The evil keeps lurking around me,
Tempting me to buy with plastic.

I don't know how it happened,
I now have two Priuses, on credit!
Well, at least they are hybrids.

But I'm not giving up,
I'm starting all over again,
Riding the bus, publishing my books.

After all, it was my love for my wife,
That caused me to buy love car #2,
Spending 50% less on gasoline.

Maybe this is round #15,
Giving credit a right knockout punch,
With Riding The Bus 1, 2, and 3!

Magical Bear (57)

Reflection: On the bus I've had the opportunities to talk to all kinds of people. I once met a young man who was on his way to see his girlfriend to say he was sorry, he was holding in his hands a stuffed bear with chocolates. I told him that I wished him well and that I would dedicate a poem for him and his girlfriend.

Magical Bear (57)

When love is born it is magical,
Sparks flow when two hearts collide,
The blood pressure rises, exhilarating,
Life seems to be beautiful, full of hope.

As love continues, mistakes are made,
Love crashes causing a multi feeling gridlock,
Yes, the blood pressure rises, causing confusion,
Life becomes complicated, love is a challenge.

The young man was holding in his hands,
A magical bear, with big wide eyes,
Although a bit over weight, he was stocked,
With chocolates, with aphrodisiac powers.

I told the young man that his bear was special,
With the power to touch a woman's heart,
I wish I had millions of cute bears to give away,
One for my wife next time she feels discouraged.

Memorable May (58)

Conveniently, the word may has two meanings: the first is the month of May and the second is a word depicting a wish, desire or permission to do something. Therefore, may the month of May be memorable in your life. May you accomplish great things during this month. May is the fifth pillar pentagonal structure of your life.

Memorable May (58)

Great things have happened this year,
January through April was great.
But here comes May, it will be better.

May all your dreams come true.
May you never forget, to continue the work,
May your friends and family progress.

This month is your fifth chance,
To do it again, try it again,
You learned and you're ready to go.

Maybe it won't be easy,
You'll have challenges along the way.
But he who persists will not desist.

Now get ready, it ain't over yet,
June is around the corner,
More ground may you cover in May.

Mexicain-coréen-français (59)

Moral : Le racisme est un thème qui apparait souvent dans mes poèmes. J'ai beaucoup souffert de l'intimidation des méchants. Comme je vous ai dit, j'avais décidé quand j'étais petit d'apprendre une troisième langue. J'ai beaucoup souffert du racisme au Mexique et aux Etats-Unis. Le racisme est une maladie qui sera avec nous pour toujours, c'est pour cela qu'on doit lutter contre l'injustice.

Mexicain-coréen-français (59)

Je suis mexicain
Avec la figure coréenne,
Et mon cœur est français.

Je suis un homme cosmopolite,
J'aime la vie, les gens, les jeunes, les vieux,
Le peuple du monde entier.

Je suis étranger n'importe où,
A la fois, citoyen du monde international,
Un qui dérange ceux qui sont racistes.

Je suis un rêveur qui croit,
Que tous sont égaux,
Que tout est possible.

Alors, je vais rêver,
Qu'un jour je serai connu,
Le poète trilingue de l'autobus international.

Molino (60)

Reflection: If you depend on others to complement you, and you give up when someone puts you down, your road to success will take a little longer. Nevertheless, it is great to have someone who believes in what you are trying to accomplish. This poem is in appreciation for a student who hasn't stop believing in me.

Molino (60)

His last name was conveniently Molina,
And "molino" is Spanish for "windmill".
As long as there was hope and a strong wind,
The molino kept encouraging and pushing.

I knew he would come and ask me,
About my next publication, next book signing,
I had to publish my next book, and finally,
I had to dedicate a poem to my mentor student.

Take time to encourage those who are trying,
And don't put them down if they are struggling.
How do you know your words are not a miracle?
Be there to give a hand, foot and arm if needed.

Therefore don't expect to be encouraged,
Don't measure yourself by other's opinions,
But I count it a blessing when my "molino"
Keeps turning and turning, encouraging, believing.

Mon père français-basque (61)

Moral: Le vrai père est celui qui s'occupe d'un enfant. Mon père biologique était absent et Dieu m'envoyé un beau vieillard, français/basque provenant de Biarritz, France. Quand j'ai grandi, peu à peu j'ai pardonné mon père natal pour son absence. Je comprends maintenant qu'il ne pouvait être parfait comme Dieu. Il faut pardonner pour être libre.

Mon père français-basque (61)

Je l'aimais comme mon propre père,
C'est lui qui m'a appris le français,
C'est lui qui m'a donné de l'espoir,
Dans un moment très dur dans ma vie.

J'étais adolescent et j'avais besoin,
D'un homme qui jouerait le rôle,
D'un père qui aimerait son fils,
Un fils à qui manquait l'amour nécessaire.

Quand il est mort, je ne voulais pas,
Accepter sa mort, mon espoir perdu,
Je voulais me souvenir de lui,
Comme un homme fort, mon héros.

Plusieurs années sont passées maintenant,
Encore aujourd'hui, il est présent dans mon esprit.
Il m'a donné un cœur français, grâce à lui,
Je suis devenu prof de français, le métier dont j'avais rêvé.

Monumental Monday (62)

Message: In Riding The Bus 3 there is a series of poems highlighting the positive side of the seven days of the week. I got the idea from a book named Mind Monsters, by Kevin Gerald. In this book he denotes the importance of having positive thoughts. I liked the idea so much that I came up with more positive things to say about the 12 months of the year.

Monumental Monday (62)

I think there are only two ways to look at life,
Manic Monday or Monumental Monday.

The first day of the week
Can be a great beginning
To a fresh new work week.

Manic Monday is boredom
Repeating last week's Monday
No hope of a better day.

Monumental Monday!
This is the day when things
Are going to change!

So, you have two choices.
This can be the same old Monday
Or the start of a great new week.

More Accidents (63)

Moral: This poem reminds me of Paul McCartney's "Silly Love Song". Here I go again just like this Beatle but this song is about being positive. I can't help it; I have to go again when you consider that negativism keeps going and going too, like an evil Duracell battery.

More Accidents (63)

Here I go again and again,
The birds are singing again,
I missed my bus again,
But the birds keep singing.

Walked twenty minutes more,
To catch the 488, birds singing,
All along the road, they keep singing.
In unison with the roaring engines.

I began to think about my life,
I have to keep singing,
In spite of all the noise,
Even if I missed my bus.

Singing again during the good times,
Singing in tune with the bad times,
Singing for hope, peace, wisdom,
I am singing my way through life.

Nania (64)

Reflection: This story has two sides and I can't finish without exposing part two. It is no coincidence that both names are magical, that they can be fused together to create two new names, two powerful names: Nania and Kency. The spray bottle incident was not enough to destroy the "castillo" (castle) of integrity and high ethics. The Bible says that we should love others as we love ourselves. Nancy loved herself enough to love Kenia even after the incident.

Nania (64)

The spray entered through her eyes
Deep into her heart and lodged
In the most inner parts of her soul.

She couldn't understand how a friendship
Had gone so stale, all communication severed.
She was willing to fix it to be friends again.

Forgiveness was in her heart
Her fortress, her "castillo" would not fall
Love always finds a way.

Fusion number two: Nancy + Kenia = Nania
As a teacher this is one of the most beautiful
The greatest miracle I have ever seen.

Some people live out their lives hating others
Not these two: they had the courage to make a difference
In the future a beautiful child will be born

And her name will be Nania.

Numerous November (65)

Moral: Life is a challenge so you have to keep focused. Take time to be thankful for the numerous blessings and victories you've had thus far. Life is too short to live regretting the past and present. Make plans so you won't regret the future. Spend less time complaining and more time improving yourself.

Numerous November (65)

This is the eleventh month of the year.
Surely you can count the blessings.
Are you still employed, healthy, alive?

Count the numerous triumphs,
You have accomplished this year,
How many battles did you win?

Number the times you worried,
And nothing bad happened,
Better count your blessings.

Number the times you won,
Learn from the times you lost,
Obviously, you're not finished yet.

So let's move forward.
Let's conquer more ground.
So we can count the numerous,
Blessings in the month of November.

Obvious October (66)

Message: This poem reminds me of my poem Nine Times, in Riding The Bus 1. The story is about a man who took a test nine times before passing it. My poem ends posing the question whether the man would have tried the test for the tenth time. The number ten is somewhat magical, leaving single digits behind. It is a symbolic of winners, people who keep trying and trying until they succeed.

Obvious October (66)

Ok, this is number ten,
And it's going to be great!
Just like September,
November even better.

This is the only way,
To think about life,
It's obvious that life,
Can be as good as you want.

Don't concentrate on the problem,
Think about the solution, act on it.
It's obvious that things can get better,
If you can get your mind to do it.

Now let's make number 10
Count for something.
It is obvious, if you work hard,
October will bring you success.

Où se trouve la gare ? (67)

Message : Je voulais toujours apprendre à parler plusieurs langues. Depuis que j'étais tout petit les autres enfants me faisaient des bêtises. Ils se moquaient de moi parce que j'avais les yeux chinois. Á vrai dire, je suis un mélange de mexicain et de coréen. Quand mes parents ont déménagé aux Etats-Unis j'avais déjà commencé à apprendre l'allemand tous simplement parce que j'habitais à Tijuana dans le quartier « Colonia Alemán » qui veut dire, colonie allemande .

Où se trouve la gare ? (67)

C'était un rêve accompli,
J'étais finalement,
Dans le pays de mon cœur.

Je venais d'arriver à Paris,
Et j'avais tellement envie,
De parler français avec quelqu'un.

Je savais où se trouvait la Gare du Nord,
Néanmoins j'ai demandé à la belle fille,
« Où se trouve la Gare du Nord » ?

C'était vraiment un rêve accompli,
J'avais travaillé plusieurs années,
Pour amasser les fonds pour mon voyage,

Tout est possible si on se le propose,
Maintenant, je lutte pour l'éducation,
Je veux la même chose pour mes étudiants.

Prendre l'autobus (68)

Message: Quand j'étais ado, la France et mon rêve m'ont sauvé. Mon père français-basque (je l'ai adopté comme père et lui, il m'a adopté comme fils) a été un guide vénérable dans les années les plus importantes dans ma vie. Mon rêve était d'apprendre une troisième langue. J'avais déjà commencé à étudier l'allemand, mais le français a gagné. ☺

Prendre l'autobus (68)

Prendre l'autobus en France,
Ça fait longtemps,
Que j'ai pris l'autobus en France,
Si longtemps que je me souviens,
Avoir été poursuivi d'un dinosaure.

Les passagers étaient tous pareils,
Comme les passagers aux États-Unis,
Des vieillards, des jeunes, des enfants,
Un jour, je le ferai encore une fois.
Je me rappelle d'une vieillarde,

Qui tremblait lorsqu'elle a vu,
L'ambulance passer devant,
De quoi avait-t-elle peur ?
Récemment j'ai commencé à visiter,
Le pays de mon cœur, que j'aime tellement,

Comme si c'était mon propre pays,
Je rêve à la retraite en France.
Et bien sûr, je vais prendre l'autobus. ☺

Primeras Lluvias (69)

Moraleja: Muchos pensamos que la lluvia es algo bueno. Los agricultores dependen de la lluvia para la siembra y la cosecha. En la ciudad la gente piensa que las calles se limpian y el aire es más limpio. Una señora en el autobús me dijo que la lluvia era buena para limpiar la suciedad de la sociedad. Me puse a pensar en tantos problemas sociales que sufre nuestra comunidad.

Primeras Lluvias (69)

Ya viene el refrescante olor de la tierra mojada
De los árboles y flores recién bañados.
Del aire filtrado por las aguas cristalinas.

Luego me puse a pensar en los problemas
Que parecen no tener solución.
Los desafíos de una sociedad decadente.

¡Qué las primeras lluvias limpiaran!
A los cholos que están en víspera
De matarse los unos a los otros.

¡Cómo quisiera! que la lluvia
Limpiara los pensamientos
De aquellos que no tienen esperanza.

¡Qué la lluvia limpiara! las calles
Que son el albergue de tantos
Hombres, mujeres y niños desamparados.

Rat's Rights (70)

Reflection: The pendulum swings in both directions. People can have no freedom or too much freedom. We shouldn't beat the child to death but we should not let him do whatever he wants. There are two extremes and we need to find a balance. Not an easy task when we consider the many beliefs and philosophies and the intolerance that sometimes accompany these values.

Rat's Rights (70)

Everyone has rights, right?
The inalienable right to pursue happiness,
The right to believe what you want.

What a waste to spend your life,
Without fighting for what you believe,
To follow the norm without passion.

But where do we draw the line?
Do women, minorities, gays, the poor,
Have the right to equal protection?

Of course they do, but what about animals?
Rats, cats, dogs, the animal kingdom,
They have the right to be left alone.

But where is the line?
Do we blow up the lab?
Kill humans to save a lab rat?

Remember September (71)

Reflection: September 23 is the first day of autumn. This day can also be the first day of your dream's unfolding. Since remember rhymes with September, maybe you should take the time again to recollect the major events of this year. How have they affected you? How did they change you? Are you a better person now, as a result of your experiences?

Remember September (71)

Autumn, the time trees start,
To shed their leaves, time to reflect.
Waiting for the first rain to fall.
To wash away the dirt and grime.

Remember the good times,
And be thankful for the blessings.
Remember the bad times,
And learn from those experiences.

September 23rd, first day of autumn,
Today, October 13th, 2013, first rainy day.
The weather is gloomy and cold,
But there's a miracle happening now.

The trees need to regenerate,
The roots and ground thirsty for,
A fresh new start, time to regenerate,
This time next year, things will be better.

Riding The Bus With Jesus (72)

Message: My future project, my fifth book, will be dedicated to Jesus, therefore there has to be an epic poem about riding the bus. I have to tell you that the time spent waiting and riding and writing are well invested. I have time to pray, to think, to write, to sleep. I couldn't write poems or sleep while driving, not to mention the money I am saving by riding the bus.

Riding The Bus With Jesus (72)

Riding the bus with Jesus,
Trusting that He is here,
Remembering the perpetual giver.

When I drove my Toyota Tacoma,
I would often wonder about people,
Cold, wet, waiting at the bus stop.

Riding the bus with Jesus, praying,
Now I know how difficult it is,
Now I am cold, wet, waiting.

"But you know, Lord"
It's not all that bad."
I still have so much to give thanks for.

Riding the bus with Jesus,
Writing my poems with Jesus,
"Thank you, Lord, for my limo.

Round #15 (73)

Message: My French-Basque father once told me a story about a general who had lost six battles and had given up. The soldier laid on his bed looking at the ceiling when he observed a spider who was trying to spin a web across the corner of the room. The spider tried six times and failed. On the seventh time the spider succeed. The general got up, determined he would win the war at the seventh battle, and he did.

Round #15 (73)

Times are hard these days.
More problems continue to arise.
Illness, more expenses, more challenges,
Have upset my plan to succeed.

I am being hit left and right,
Negativism punching out my daylights,
Positivism bending under the pressure,
Losing faith in self and others.

I can't see, my eyes are obscured,
My legs heavy with pain and fatigue,
My arms and shoulders drained,
But I'm not giving up!

I hear the words of Rocky Balboa,
"What's important in not how hard
You hit, but how hard you get hit,
And still remain standing", round 15 is here!

Running Again (74)

Message: Since I have been going through stuff I have been neglecting bus riding. I have been going to bed late and getting up a little later, enough for me to resort to love car #1, my Prius. Sometimes when we make a commitment, we have to try it again and again.

Running Again (74)

I am going through "stuff" right now,
Aren't we all at one point or another?
I missed the pleasure of writing,
Let others do the driving, while I sleep.

I feel rejuvenated this morning,
Running again to catch my limo!
Getting my daily forced exercise,
Again, pushing toward debt freedom.

I missed the naps, conversations,
I missed stretching my legs,
Rolling my neck, flexing my back,
Arms reaching the sky, "busercising",

A new commitment, again and again,
Pushing harder against my struggles,
Having faith in my dreams, my goals,
I feel so good, I'm running again!

Sacrifices (75)

Reflection: If you want to accomplish something in life you have to make sacrifices. Students have to sacrifice time and sleep. Parents have to sacrifice money and vacations if they want their children to go to college. Life itself is a sacrifice. We have to make decisions.

Sacrifices (75)

Sacrifices are a way of life,
Everyone sacrifices for something,
Making sacrifices for those things,
That are important to us.

Working long hours, riding the bus,
Sacrificing time, making effort,
Taking the difficult road,
That leads to a better place.

Riding the bus, to save money,
To pay for my son's violin lessons,
To pay for my daughter's art lessons,
Riding the bus to bless others.

My wife working seven days a week,
Sacrificing time, rest, sleep,
My son sacrificing to practice on his violin,
My daughter sacrificing to graduate from Parsons.

Sacrifices have to be made to acquire gain.

Sans amour (76)

Espoir : Voici une chanson que j'ai écrite d'abord en espagnol à l'âge de 25 ans et puis je l'ai traduite en français. Vous pouvez me trouver sur YouTube. Amusez-vous bien.

Sans amour (76)

Sans amour,
Il n'y a pas raison,
Il n'y a pas saison,
Vivre sans amour.

Même les papillons,
Même les fleurs,
Nulle personne,
Vivra sans amour.

Je trouverai,
Quelque part,
Un amour qui soit,
Fait pour moi.

Un amour qui,
Me rende heureux,
Je trouverai,
Quelque part,

Un amour qui,
Soit fait pour moi,
Un amour qui,
Me rende heureux.

Satisfying Saturday (77)

Message: For some people Saturday is a sacred day, for others it's a party weekend. For others Saturday can be just as bad or good as the day before, expecting the best or the worst the day after. It all depends how you see the world. It's up to you if you seek out the good or the bad in things.

Satisfying Saturday (77)

For some Saturday is sacred,
Others, another day of work.
I say Saturday is satisfying.
A day for rest, to accomplish goals.

The sixth day for some,
The seventh day for others.
I suggest every day is great!
It all depends how you see it.

Things to do, people to visit,
Relax, go to church perhaps.
Whatever you do, enjoy it.
May it be something productive.

Think positive, satisfying, sensational,
Successful, supernatural, sensible,
Saving, sensual maybe, why not?
Be careful though, Saturday can also,

Thyme with "I Sat-all-day" ☺.

Sauna Bus (78)

Message: Riding a tin can during a scorching hot day can be excruciating. This was one of those days when the air-conditioning should not break down. Murphy won this one, "If the air conditioner can break down, it will". I tried to stay positive: I was on a sauna bus.

Sauna Bus (78)

Life is really hard for some people.
The choice of comfort is not their own.
Riding the bus by necessity not choice.

The temperature was over 100 Fahrenheit,
Sweat coming down my forehead,
Sauna bus for only a buck fifty,

I remembered the sauna at 24 Hour Fitness,
When the economy was doing great,
Thought money would never run out.

Then came the crash of 2007
I wasn't prepared for what was to come,
Credit could no longer be a way of life,

The heat got unbearable, no air-conditioning,
Bus driver goes to the back to close all windows,
Said open windows were truncating the engine.

Couldn't take it anymore,
Got off the bus, called my wife,
For a well-deserved ride.

Setbacks 3 (79)

Reflection: I said it once and I have to say it again and again. Life is full of challenges and full of winners. The winners are those who never give up and if the fall they come back. You may be going throw a difficult time now, but remember; it won't last forever. When this challenge if over, you'll look back and laugh.

Setbacks 3 (79)

Funny thing, this is Riding The Bus 3,
Setbacks continue, but so do the dream,
Three setbacks, six steps forward.

Life is a series of ups and downs,
But we have to remember the ups,
If we want to move forward.

Forget the downs, they are lessons,
Only remember the past to learn,
Avoid making the same mistakes.

This is Riding The Bus 3, no giving up.
I am going to start all over again,
Keep keeping on till I win.

Anybody can give up,
Winners seek out new opportunities,
Setbacks never set them back.

She Cried (80)

Moral: As a teacher, a husband, a parent, at times I may feel that I'm not doing my best. I want to do more and I want to accomplish goals that I thought were impossible. Sometimes God sends a person, an angel to assure that you are doing great. God sent ma student that made me feel that my best was good enough. Her tears made me feel that I was doing the right thing.

She Cried (80)

"Your poems are so beautiful Mr."
Fanning herself with her hand,
As to dry up her weeping eyes.

They say tears clean up the soul,
Tears of joy, sorrow and despair,
Too many of us hold them back.

Not my student, she cried.
Not Jesus, he cried too,
When told Lazarus had died.

Graduation is coming up.
Perhaps there will be more tears,
I want to be there to give a big hug.

Jesus, be with her next time she cries.

Singing Again (81)

Moral: Again, I have to say this again, and yet I can't say it enough. It is really difficult to stay positive especially during the bad times. The struggles in our lives are like gravity pulling down the aircraft. The only way an airplane can soar into the sky is by emitting a force superior to that of gravity.

Singing Again (81)

Here I go again and again,
The birds are singing again,
I missed my bus again,
But the birds keep singing.

Walked twenty minutes more,
To catch the 488, birds singing,
All along the road, they keep singing.
In unison with the roaring engines.

I began to think about my life,
I have to keep singing,
In spite of all the noise,
Even if I missed my bus.

Singing again during the good times,
Singing in tune with the bad times,
Singing for hope, peace, wisdom,
I am singing my way through life.

Start All Over Again (82)

Message: In the world of winners often times things have to get done more than once to reach perfection. The concept of doing things again and again is the key to success. If you are trying to do something and you fail, do it again and again. Every time you learn from your mistakes and it's a matter of time before you accomplish what others thought impossible.

Start All Over Again (82)

The budget didn't work this month.
Debt seems to be increasing, getting bigger.
It's ok, I'm going to start all over again.

If life was easy, anybody would do it right,
Things that are worth anything take time.

Had to buy another car on credit,
It's ok, I'm starting all over again,
Too easy to give up, anyone can give up.

I'm not giving up on my dream,
I will be totally debt free, credit free.
Free from the hassle of installments.

Therefore, if the going gets tough,
Don't give up, keep trying, how do you know?
That the next one won't be the charm?

Terrific Tuesday (83)

Reflection: Thinking positive is not easy. On the other hand, it is so easy to be negative. I have found that I have to push myself to think that Tuesday can be terrific. I believe that thinking negative is more natural for most people. Thinking positive is a life-time commitment.

Terrific Tuesday (83)

People like to find words
That rhyme with terrible.
The terrible two's, terrible Tuesday.

Well. Terrible also rhymes with terrific.
I'd like to think that Tuesday is terrific!
The second day, better than the first.

Terrific Tuesday, fighting for good.
For hope, for progress and dreams,
The terrifying truth that dreams can come true!

A war between terrific and terrible.
Which of the two will stand in the end?
The difference is you, what you believe.

Test Of Fire (84)

Message: I remember watching a scene in one of the Super Man series where Clark Kent takes a pile of coal, squeezes it with all his strength and a large diamond emerges. I wish someone would take me squeeze me really hard, only problem, I am not made of coal. Nonetheless, I believe that challenges I have had in my life have molded me into the person I am today.

Test Of fire (84)

Coal endures high pressure,
For millions of years,
Then the diamond is born!

Gold is purified,
Under extreme heat,
And a hot kitchen smells good!

Life is a series of trials,
Tribulation is a way of life,
The test of fire, purification.

How long will life press upon a man?
How much will the heat of life burn?
How long before she is transformed?

Remember, if you are under fire and pressure,
Hold on! Be steadfast, strong, have faith,
Wait till the diamonds and gold emerge!

Thank You, Lord (85)

Moral: Complaining and asking for more is human phenomenon. As a general rule we humans are not satisfied with what we have. I began to think about showing gratitude for the things we take for granted. Have you heard of the Indian proverb that says?, "I once thought I had it bad because I didn't have shoes until I met a man who never had feet."

Thank You, Lord (85)

"In all things give thanks"
The bible makes reference
To the simple concept of gratitude.

The economy is uncertain,
People speak of the end of time.
Irregular weather patterns, earthquakes,

Then I began thinking,
Thanking God for anything,
Thank you Lord, for everything.

Thank you for my eyes,
Thank you for my feet, my hands,
Thank you for my ears and mouth.

The list of "thank you things"
Would not fit in one book.
Thank you for the crack on the sidewalk,
Where I once fell and got up again.

The Good Mexican (86)

In the times of Jesus, the Jews were not supposed to associate with the Samaritans. To this day in some remote part of the country there may still be people who will say, don't talk to Mexicans or Blacks. Racism is as old as humanity. Envy, the desire to have more than one's neighbor will never end.

The Good Mexican (86)

The Jews and the Samaritans were not friends,
The Samaritans had been branded with lies,
In the Bible there are stories of good dealings,
Between Jesus and the Samaritans.

I thought of the parable of the good Samaritan,
Then I imagined the parable of the good Mexican.
What would Jesus do if he met up with a Mexican?
Would he judge him through stereotypes?

Then I thought of the Samaritan woman at the well,
Would you accept a cold glass of water? Jesus did.
Therefore if Jesus thought that the despised Samaritans,
Were cool enough to be accepted by him,

I challenge you to find a Good Mexican,
Don't hire him to cut your lawn, prune your bushes,
Don't have her clean your house, watch your kids,
Invite him/her into your house to be friends.

Maybe that's why they don't speak English.

The Big 1 "O" (87)

Message: Just after I turned 50, my son turned 10. Those days were so precious! I was my son's hero. We did all kinds of stuff together: karate, carwash, pool, basketball and more. I knew my son would never see a single digit again.

The Big 1 "O" (87)

My big 5 "O" party had just passed,
And I knew the big 1 "O" was at hand.
It would be the last time my son,
Would ever see a single digit.

"Time to get you back", I said.
I threw a big "O" party for him.
Friends, neighbors and a big "O" family.

Unforgettable party, presents galore,
My wife and I, proud of our son,
His sister, jealous for all his gifts.

I was my son's hero,
I was the smartest guy he knew,
But then he grew up.

Things were changing.
He wanted to spend more time alone,
I became busy with school,
My son will always be my hero.

The Dream Continues (88)

Message: You know why the dream continues? Because the problems continue. There is up and down, left and right, strong and weak, therefore the dream has to continue. There has to be an equal or stronger force than evil to maintain a balance. If you have negative thoughts you should also have positive thoughts. Please feed your positive thoughts more so that good will prevail.

The Dream Continues (88)

That's right! The dream continues.
What else could continue, the problems?
No! Struggle till you win, find the solution.

It's so easy to give up, to stop trying,
Anybody can give up, throw in the towel,
Only the true, strong and mighty survive.

But let's not just survive, barely make it,
Let's thrive! Drive toward our dream!
Having faith, making it happen.

Anybody who ever did anything,
Never gave up, until it was finished,
Therefore the dream must continue!

So I am going to go out there!
Continue riding the bus, writing my poems,
Looking for people to bless and bless me back!

The Final Test (89)

Moral: Life is full of tests. Sometimes we are not prepared and we just have to look back to see where we made mistakes. Look at these life lessons as a preparation for events to come. You will be better prepared to take the test courageously and triumphantly.

The Final Test (89)

When things were great,
You never thought,
It would get this way.

You became a victim of circumstances,
You didn't plan for future emergencies,
The fallen economy caught you by surprise.

Now the question remains,
Are you going to pass the final test?
Things are tough, will you be rough?

The final test, how will you walk tall again?
Have you been humbled enough to realize,
That sometimes you need help?

Now prove that you are worthy of the test.
Take out your notes, life lessons,
Not the first time or last time you had a test.

The Little Things (90)

Reflection: Elizabeth Berg an accomplished poet and novelist once said that it is those random moments, arbitrary moments that make up her life. Such things as tossing a salad or driving up the driveway of her house seemed quite insignificant while still part of the big picture. We humans need to learn to appreciate the little things in our life so that we can see clearly.

The Little things (90)

It's the little things,
That matter in life,
Like Elizabeth Berg stated of,
"The flimsy heads of dandelions,
Voices and coins in an open field.

It's the little things in life,
That can virtually open the mind,
Things that are seemingly insignificant,
Can open a world of imagination.

A dead rose on the ground,
Has a story to tell,
A quiet student has a lot to say,
I hope someday he will speak.

Little things can be big,
You are born, grow and die,
Pay attention to the little things.
You'll understand big things better.

The Race Of Life (91)

Message: Drug abuse is out of control. People are using drugs to escape reality. A nephew of mine was a victim of circumstance. He felt he didn't belong in this world and he took refuge in drugs. If you have problems and insecurities don't resort to more problems, get help. Don't be ashamed to accept that you have a problem.

The Race Of Life (91)

He grew up in a world,
That was not his own.
He often said that,
He didn't belong in this world.

Life is a race to get ahead,
A race for money, status,
Some pursue a higher education,
Others steal, sell pain and despair.

He and two other friends were,
Dare devils, defying life itself.
His life took a bad turn,
A race with a fatal train.

The morning paper read,
"Train race, two men win, one loses".
The final game of life where,
No one comes out alive.

Thriving Thursday (92)

Message: Can I talk too much about positive thinking? I don't think so. There are too many soldiers of negativism out there. There needs to be a positive force to counteract the bad vibes. Negative thinking probably far outweighs positive thoughts. Fortunately, I believe, a good thought can most likely wipeout 100 doomsday thoughts.

Thriving Thursday (92)

A day to continue Wednesday's progress.
The rest of the week to thrive.
On Thursday my roller coaster goes up!

Striving Thursday, starting new projects.
Finishing yesterday's work, planning Friday.
No day good enough to give up.

Thriving Thursday, hope and rewarding work,
Expecting only the best, thrust forward.
Through the day at full throttle.

A day to trust, to try new things.
Now I am excited for tomorrow,
Can't wait the arrival of Fruitful Friday.

Time To March (93)

Reflection: March is the third month of our Gregorian calendar, a lucky number for some people. It is my birthday month, therefore a special one. Nevertheless, this month like others I plan to accomplish much. This month marks new beginnings, with the onset of Spring. It is a month to continue thinking positive, that dreams can come true. Keep working toward your goal and your labor will not be in vain.

Time To March (93)

March is finally here.
Time to march, to move forward.
Another chance to do it right.

March like a soldier toward your mark.
March in harmony like the high school band.
March toward your goal, don't waver.

March 20th, the first day of Spring,
Time to spring back into action.
To finish and improve projects, your life.

New seeds, flowers, plants forming roots,
The harvest of January and February is here.
To enjoy the fruit of your labor.

True To Yourself (94)

Reflection: Again, I am sorry I am doing this again. Some things you just can't say enough even if you think you are overdoing it. The personal inner drive that an individual has is never ending. Most things take years and several trials before perfection is reached.

True To Yourself (94)

Again, the concept arises,
Are you going to give up?
Are you going to try again?

If a problem arises,
Will you also rise and stand?
Will you bend under the pressure?

You have to be true to yourself,
Fight to keep the dream alive,
Fight to conquer the giant.

Discover who you truly are,
It's during the hard times,
When the real you comes out.

Ok, now you know who you are.
Now go out there and do it again,
Again and again until you get it right!

Trust In The Lord (95)

Reflection: In life there are many challenges along with uncertainties. At times we may fear the outcome of a certain event. Marriage, children employment and the economy can change out lives in drastic ways. We have to trust the Lord that all these things will work out in the end.

Trust In The Lord (95)

Trust in the Lord with all your heart.
I trust you Lord with my wife,
I trust you with my daughter in New York.
I trust you with my son at LACHSA.

I trust you with the progress of my students.
I trust you with next year's class assignment.
I trust you with the establishment of my 501 (c) 3.
I trust you with our trip to Europe.

The economy is really bad these days,
There is talk about closing adult school,
There is talk about laying off more teachers,
I trust you to keep my job.

Sometimes things may not work out,
More than ever, I have to trust in You,
Yesterday we received a counterfeit 20,
I have to trust you Lord.

Two Wheelchairs (96)

Moral: The Bible says that we should not ask signs from God, but sometimes it's ok to ask for little miracles, such as two wheelchairs. My first bus was late so I had to walk-run to catch a different route. Walking and running would not have been enough so I asked God for two wheelchairs. I knew that two wheelchairs would slow down the bus about five minutes, just enough to for me to catch the bus. Low and behold, there was two wheelchairs on the bus when I got on.

Two Wheelchairs (96)

Walk-running, panting, sweating,
At 6am to catch the late bus,
I'm running again and I won't stop.

I know the road ahead is hard,
But I can't stop if I want to win,
Pushing forward, lugging my bags.

"Lord, Jesus, if you could only give me,
Two wheelchairs to slow down the bus,
Enough to make my efforts worthwhile.

"I know the bearded librarian
Got off that bus, he's not on the road."
Finally I reached my stop, just in time.

I got on the bus exhilarated,
Elated to find two wheelchairs and,
The bearded librarian out the back door.

Un Champurrado (97)

Moraleja: Muchos de los inmigrantes que venimos a Los Ángeles venimos a trabajar con el alma. Buscamos una vida mejor para nosotros y nuestras familias. Algunos abrimos negocios, otros trabajamos duro. Otros optan por estudiar como yo, profesor de español y francés, su servidor. Lamento por aquellos que vienen a fracasar, pero nunca es tarde. ¡A levantarse y a comenzar de nuevo!

Un Champurrado (97)

Muy temprano, en el fresco de la mañana,
Me aproximé al puestito de tamales y champurrado.
"Traigo un coraje, ¿qué me recomienda?".
"Pues un champurrado" me dice orgullosamente.

Yo admiro a los eloteros, los paleteros,
A todos los que tienen un puesto en la calle.
Bien tempranito como el pájaro madrugador.
Admiro su tenacidad, el deseo de trabajar.

"Ando bien contento esta mañana.
¿Qué le quedaría bien a mi alegría?"
 "Un champurrado, me contesta con una sonrisa."
Un champurrado, un cúralo todo.

"Qué es bueno para un poeta?"
"Un champurrado, por supuesto!"
"Écheme, pues, un tamal de queso
Para que sea completo el pecado."

Un Milagro (98)

Moraleja: Todos queremos lograr metas en la vida. Algunos nunca se dan por vencidos y lo logran. Otros se ven acarreados por el costo de la vida. Solamente aquellos que descubren que la fuerza está en nuestras manos llegan lejos. En mi poema quiero dar a entender que lo imposible es posible. Yo sé que a veces no podemos lograr todas nuestras metas pero si no le tiramos a lo lejos tampoco llegaremos cerca.

Un Milagro (98)

Necesito un milagro.
Estudiantes que quieran superarse
Profesores que no le tengan
Miedo al riesgo.

Necesito un milagro.
Estudiantes que aprendan
Que sus errores sean su maestro
Que se miren en espejo.

Necesito un milagro
Pensadores, sonadores, conquistadores
Para ir a lugares donde nuestros
Antepasados sonaron sonar.

Necesito un milagro
Yo soy el milagro
Todos somos milagros
Tu reflexión en el espejo de tus sueños.

Veinte Dólares (99)

Moraleja: El dinero en sí, no tiene valor. Todo depende como lo usamos, en que lo invertimos. Veinte dólares se pueden emplear para ayudar a un pobre o para comprar droga y destruir la vida de una persona. Este relato se trata de un hombre que usó su dinero para algo bueno. Verdaderamente no sabemos el valor de estos veinte dólares.

Veinte Dólares (99)

Su amigo le pidió cinco dólares prestados,
Se los prestó acompañado de un consejo.
"ya deja de tomar por tu propio bien.
Pasó tiempo sin verlo, luego la sorpresa.

"Aquí están tus cinco dólares y 15 de pilón.
Esta cantidad no se compara con el dineral
Que él tiraba a la taza del baño, los árboles.
El amigo había dejado el trago, agradecido.

Pero la historia no termina aquí.
Esos veinte tenían un destino
Me tocaban a mí, una bendición.
A dónde mas ira Mr. Jackson?

Con orgullo tomé los veinte
Y le entregué mi libro "Riding The Bus"
Junto con un centavo de buena suerte
¿Adónde irá ese centavito?

Walk n'Roll (100)

Message: I said it once, I'll say it again. There are only two ways to look at life: you can be positive or you can be positive. This a story about a woman I met on the bus who confirmed in my heart that we have to be happy. Weeks later I met the woman and she introduced me to her husband, a freelance musician.

Walk n'Roll (100)

I asked God for two wheelchairs,
And he gave them to me,
I made it just in time.

A woman on a wheelchair,
Who told me joke after joke,
The wheelchair did not hold her back.

Weeks later, her walking husband,
A freelance musician with a dream,
"This is my husband, together we walk and roll".

This woman had my undivided attention,
She had jokes about rabbits, paranoid men,
She had the pessimists on their toes.

Finally I arrived at my stop,
And I had to ask her, "Mam, has anyone,
Ever told you, you are on a wheelchair?"

Waz Up Dawg? (101)

Message: It is sad how so many mental health people go untreated. On the public bus, in supermarkets, schools, churches, just about anywhere we will meet people who are suffering from depression or other psychological illnesses. This a story about a retried "veterano" who gave me a rather interesting surprise.

Waz Up Dawg? (101)

"Waz up Dawg"? the veterano greeted,
As my limousine approached its stop.
"You get in first Dawg", as he racked his bike.
"I'm a Christian and that's how I roll".

"Well that's great sir, I'm a Christian too."
He proceeded to tell me his business.
He was on his way to the drug store to buy,
Flowers for his wife, match made in heaven.

He continued to share about his wife,
Yea, Dawg. My wife is a college professor,
She has been at ELAC for the longest.
That's really interesting sir, congratulations.

He caught me off guard, proceeded
To tell me he was currently homeless,
"I asked him, what about your wife?"

"What's wrong with me being homeless Dawg?
Bus driver, let me off! This Dawg is snarling,
Is snarling his teeth at me."

What Would Jesus Do? (102)

Reflection: I once had an acquaintance, a friend who would ask me, "What would Jesus do?" when he wanted a favor from me. I would usually try to get away, especially if I was busy. But then he would pose the question and I would drop whatever I was doing and give him a hand. Then things changed, he moved to another school and I have not heard from him since.

What Would Jesus Do? (102)

I was in the middle of something,
And I got the call, he needed help,
I was busy at the time, but then,
He would drop the question.

To him, perhaps it was a game,
I took it seriously; What would Jesus do?,
I dropped whatever I was doing,
I could finish it later.

He needed the popcorn maker,
for a fundraiser for his mother's church,
I needed the magic machine too,
But Jesus would let him use the machine first.

So the question remains, What would Jesus do?
Whether you think he was the savior or God,
Most everyone will agree that he was a nice guy.
But here is another question, What will you do?

Who Are You? (103)

Message: When I go through hard times, sometimes I just want to give up, or just stop and take a break. When things are great, many people don't stop to plan for emergencies. We think that it is always going to be easy. The fallen economy caught the world by surprise. We used credit like candy and had little or no savings. I am one of those who fell victim to the world of credit.

Who Are You? (103)

When things are great,
You think you know who you are.
When you go through struggles,
You find out who you really are.

Who are you when things go wrong?
When it's your turn to lose?
Who are you when odds are against you?
When it's time to stand?

Who are you, when all seems lost?
When you run out of options?
Will you keep trying and trying?
Will your problems weigh you down?

I know who I am,
The struggles of my life have taught me,
My character has been shaped,
Whenever you fall, get up and go again!

That's who you really are.

Woman On The Floor (104)

Moral: This is a sad story about a homeless woman I met at a bus stop. She was laying on the sidewalk and she screamed out for help as I walked by. I pulled her to her feet and helped her sit on her wheelchair. Then she asked me to give her water and 4 pills. I wish I could have done more but my bus had just arrived.

Woman On The Floor (104)

"Help! Will someone help me?"
"I don't have any money mam,"
I really didn't have any money on me.

"No, you don't understand sir,
I have been here on the floor,
All day and I can't get up.

Her hands and feet were swollen with sores,
I was afraid to touch her, in fear of infection,
But I did it anyway, trusting my fate.

"Can you help me take my meds?,
You're the only one who offered to help,
They dropped me off here with no shoes.

Some might say I was a good Samaritan,
I say I was just at the right place,
At the right time to make a difference.

Wonderful Wednesday (105)

Message: The middle of the week for many is Wednesday. People say it is downhill from that point on. I wonder if they mean that from a positive point of view or if they are just anxious to see the end of the week. I believe that the day before, today and tomorrow all hold promises.

Wonderful Wednesday (105)

Wonderful, fruitful, flourishing,
Wishful, wisdom, wellness, wealth.
Ok, that's enough rhythm with wonderful.

Wining Wednesday, no, just kidding.
I am about being positive, not negative.
Finding the good in things.

Too many people look for the negative.
Hump Wednesday, over the hill,
After a hard beginning, not me.

I'm going up, keep climbing.
Can't wait till Thursday,
A thriving Thursday, day of triumph.

Riding The Bus 3

ABOUT THE AUTHOR

Mr. Luis Pástor continues in his quest to become a renowned writer and publisher of motivational poetry. He is a teacher of French and Spanish with almost 30 years of experience. He is persistent in his dream to have a working 501 (c) 3, Youth World Clean Up, (formerly EFIST International) that will have the purpose of giving students a vision of educational/international travel and a desire to further their education. Be on the lookout and expect more from this aspiring author. Thank you for your support.
For your comments please email ridingthebus1@yahoo.com. Also email me if you would like me to go to your organization as a motivational speaker and to conduct a book signing. To order more books go to the following websites:
Riding The Bus 1: www.createspace.com/4351776
Riding The Bus 2: www.createspace.com/4263297
Riding The Bus 3: www.createspace.com/4630433

Thank you for your patronage.

Made in the USA
Columbia, SC
04 June 2025

58745683R00078